THREE LETTERS

Lothair I,
Holy Roman Emperor

Translated by: D.P. Curtin

Dalcassian Publishing Company
PHILADELPHIA, PA

THREE LETTERS

Copyright @ 2011 Dalcassian Publishing Company

All rights reserved. No part of this publication may be reproduced, distributed, or transmitted in any form or by any means, including photocopying, recording, or other electronic or mechanical methods, without the prior written permission of the publisher, except in the case of brief quotations embodied in critical reviews and certain other non-commercial uses permitted by copyright law. For permission request, write to Dalcassian Publishing Company at dalcassianpublishing at gmail.com

ISBN: 979-8-8691-2669-6 (Paperback)

Library of Congress Control Number:
Author: Curtin, D.P. (1985-)

Printed by Ingram Content Group, 1 Ingram Blvd, La Vergne, Tennessee

First printing edition 2011.

THREE LETTERS

Epistle I. First letter to Nicholas, Pope

It is conquered that the pontiff believes too much of himself for his rivals. He expresses his sorrow for the excommunication of Theutgaud and Guntharius. Purging himself of everything else, he showed himself ready to refute the slanders of his adversaries before the pontiff.

To the truly blessed and most holy lord of the whole holy church of God, to the supreme pontiff and universal pope Nicolaus, Lotharius, by divine foreboding clemency, king, peace and glory of the highest happiness and present prosperity.

After the divine condescension entrusted us with his gratuitous clemency the governors of the kingdom, in the manner of our predecessors most Christian kings, we have always and in all things exalted the seat of the blessed Peter the

Apostle, the prince, as it is worthy, we reverently loved it, and urgently, as far as it is in us, we are ready to exalt it, and with yours as always desiring to draw salubriousness from the supreme spiritual rule of the Father, we recall what was said to you by the voice of truth: Peter, do you love me? feed my sheep (John 11); and through the prophet: I will feed my sheep, says the Lord God: I will seek that which was lost, and that which was cast away I will bring back, and that which was broken I will bind up, and that which was weak I will strengthen (Ez. 34). Indeed, we long to present our presence to you more quickly, so that you can fill it with a truer experience, which the same prophet added a little later: And I will judge them in judgment and justice. Indeed, the most serene and most devout affection of your pious paternity clouded our minds sharply, because we believed too much in the false voices of our rivals, beyond what was necessary for us, in our derogation of your most holy apostleship we listened to. Especially since our meekness is most ready to resist every detractor of the truth and with just reason: which also your ambassadors, lately directed in these parts, could intimate to you if they wished, because we had given our accusers firm access to come, and a reasonable satisfaction, as in your patience. We were prepared to comply with the instructions from your side, not favoring our royal dignity, but as one of the baser persons, under the priestly admonitions of our parents. Our rivals, understanding all this with a sinister interpretation, were inflamed in their lust for the kingdom granted to us by divine condescension by hereditary right: not heeding the Scripture which says: The kingdom is the Lord's, and to whomsoever He will He will give it (Dan. 4): nor the Apostle who said: There is no power but from God (Rom. 13). Therefore the right hand of that victor for us, as we believe, fighting, who knows both the plunderer and the one who is plundered, we despise their disguised similitudes: only as an anchor of your pontificate, fixed in the most solid foundation of the holy mother Church, it is designed to grant to those who similarly ask us what in the commandments with the finger It is read in God's writings: Judge your neighbor justly (Lev. 19). Moreover, while we were staying almost at the extreme ends of our kingdom, and keeping laborious guards against the invasion of the heathen, we found, by the report of those who had fled, Theutgaud of Treviri, and Guntharius of Agrippina, excommunicated by your authority, and canonically condemned by the testimony of their own mouths; I have been told to bear patiently and patiently, and as has been done in many cases in the past, to have the hope of restitution, and after you have piously refreshed and reconsidered all, a place of reasonable mercy will be prepared by your generosity. In the meantime it happened to us to know that Guntharius was not afraid to celebrate the solemnities of the masses before he reached us, and, according to the previous custom, to make the episcopal chrism, and to deliver the Spirit to the paraclete; . But when he came to us, we did not want to hear his mass, nor did we decide to communicate with him in anything, and according to the voice of Truth, as if it were an offending eye, we determined to remove the stain from us, until such time as your most holy apostolate should be able to rescind the final sentence about him. We have also transmitted to him a letter directed by your holiness to the diocesan bishops, so that, knowing clearly the canonical and apostolic sanctions, he may see what he should do in the future. Of the rest, let your fatherhood truly and sincerely know that Theutgaudus, the most simple and innocent man, humbly bearing your censure, presumed to have nothing to do with the sacred ministry, choosing rather to suffer dishonor in the sight of men, than to be separated from the members of him who is the head of the humble by disobedience, and he said to his disciples: Learn from me because I am gentle and humble in heart, and you will find rest for your souls (Matt. 11). For he who resists the proud, and gives grace to the lowly, will be able, if he is innocent, to look down on him with mercy from above. Indeed, we commanded our ambassadors Theutgaud and Guntharius to do nothing of the sort in their embassy, from which they would incur the mark of condemnation. But neither should we nor wish to bear any prejudice against Ingeltrude, Boson's wife: as we, finding that she was bound by the bond of anathema, commended Guntharius, because he was then in his parish, admonishing him to do his service concerning her, nay, she from all the ends of our kingdom. We decided to eliminate it. For your ambassadors, requiring that latter method, and deciding in the middle, we do not know what end they imposed on the cause itself. But the diocesan bishops of the metropolis of Trier, and of the colony of Agrippina, will be proved to be neither accomplices of the damned, nor supporters of vices, nor in any respect contemptors of apostolic decrees, or violators of canonical dogmas, but worshipers of the sound and catholic faith and the truth of God. Therefore, for the sake of God, the holy and individual Trinity, we humbly ask that you will by no means admit criminals easily to our cause: nor, as the Apostle teaches, believe every spirit, but prove whether it is from God (1 John 4): for we are ready, if reason dictates , to polish by ourselves, that which the envy of rivals pretends to be alien. May Almighty God keep your most holy prince safe and sound for a long time. Amen.

Epistle II. To the same

In order to escape the threatened excommunication on account of his association with Waldrada, he announces his arrival at Rome to Nicholas, and in order to entertain him with the good hopes of the bishops, resolves to send him an embassy, and promises him help against the Saracens, if need be.

To the truly most holy and blessed Lord, and to the whole Church of God, acquired by the pink blood of the pious King Christ, the supreme pontiff and universal pope, Nicolaus, Lotharius, by divine propitiatory clemency, your king and most devoted son, everlasting glory with joy, prosperity and happiness, and faithful service.

Christ, king of kings and chief of shepherds, who united in himself the priestly and royal dignity in the ministry of our redemption, and who entrusted the care of his flock to the blessed Peter, the prince of the apostles, he established us with wholesome edicts, that we may faithfully love your apostolate, the most sacred pinnacle divinely sublimated at the foundation of the Church , and we will worship humbly. Hence it is that the feelings of our meekness are kindled by the fire of true charity around your highness, and for many days past, it has not ceased to invite us to your presence with desirability. Wherefore we direct these tips to your most eminent paternity, that we may speedily recover from your desirable longing, which is more precious than the luster of all jewels and is embraced in our body as a treasure dearer to us. And because we firmly believe the same thing about your health, we have decided rather to intimate to you, that by divine mercy, our meekness flourishes best, and the generality of our faithful in the necessary affairs of the republic, relying on Christ, will have healthy growths, indeed, the success of prosperity will benefit from him who is the giver of all goods. humbly and faithfully, we pray. Know also that the kingdom entrusted to us by divine mercy from all the invasion of the pagans, and the depredations of other enemies, with the right hand of Almighty God fighting for us and supported by the merits of the blessed Peter the Apostle, and supported by your almighty prayers, know that until now it remains safe with all integrity.

Moreover, let the pious fatherhood of your holiness know that at this time we have the most fervent desire to visit the thresholds of the apostles' prayer, and to see your long-desired face, and to sweetly embrace your sacred footsteps; and already for the second and third time of our journey we have rehearsed the equipment under a certain decision, which remains in the wish of those wishing to fulfill it. It is true that if any variety of perilous times, which is far away, should interrupt our vow, we will endeavor to appoint our ambassadors Gutfrid [Luitfrid] our dearest uncle, and Walter our faithful, as well as Theutgaud the venerable archbishop, and Atton, so that through them your highness may clearly know how faithful we are to you in everything, we and our faithful, and how faithfully we desire to obey your wholesome counsels and spiritual admonitions. Indeed, as a spiritual and most devout son of the most reverend father, and the universal pope, he must, since we and our venerable bishops and faithful, if not in body, at least in heart, have moved to your sacred footsteps, we humbly ask that if any of our enemies on our side, something sinister he has presumed to signify to your most holy ears, like a serpentine virus, the apostolic authority abominable by the false praise of falsehood. And indeed, our bishops, disciples of the truth, cannot be teachers of error, who will be proved to be true worshipers of the orthodox father of the Catholic and apostolic faith.

Among these things we have thought it proper to insert, that if any incursion of the pagans has attempted to enter the borders entrusted to you by the blessed Peter the heavenly, or perhaps has presumed to break into the borders of the most august emperor and the most beloved of our Germans, Louis, as we have found in the most recent and unfortunate report, that this should be reported to us without any delay we ask because by every postponing loss of temporal things, and by the trifling destruction of the kingdom, for the love and fear of God, and the reverence of the blessed apostles, and of all the saints, and at the same time for your most holy fatherhood, which we have resolved to love and venerate above all mortals, we and our faithful ones are in danger of death and danger we are ready to surrender, knowing that it is written: We must not fear death, which without doubt leads to life.

Therefore, with the strength of our vows, let us implore the mercy of the Lord, that our meekness may at last be represented by the safety of your most excellent alms; in so far as a truer experience of your apostolate can clearly know whether the utterances have emanated from the source of truth. Our almighty God will preserve and exalt the memory of your most holy pontificate, the pinnacle of success marked by successful successes for the protection of the flock, most gloriously and most eminently father.

Epistle III. To Pope Adrian II

Lotharius, having been informed of the death of Nicholas, writes these letters to his successor Adrian, asking him to obtain from him what he could not obtain from Nicholas, his coming to Rome.

To the most holy and most blessed Adrian, supreme pontiff and universal pope, Lothar, by divine foreboding clemency, king, peace and glory of eternal bliss and present prosperity.

The unfortunate report, and hitherto remaining in doubt, so to speak, has sharply shaken the ears of our serenity by informing us that the Lord Nicholas, universal pope of blessed memory, has departed from this vale of tears, calling Christ, to be crowned with the saints, as we believe, inestimably. Wherefore the affection of our meekness, groaning exceedingly, is shaken with a twin sorrow, that is to say, that the mother of all the Churches of God, the holy and apostolic Church, loved such and such a father, and in the heavenly Jerusalem is a lamp burning and shining in our perilous times from the dark ends of the wickedness of God [day] removed Nor does it differ that every Christian religion mourns over such a pontiff, and every ecclesiastical order groans over the wisest and most holy pope. Indeed, let us rather weep, who have committed the unusual causes of our slander, and the fraudulent complaints of our rivals, to be weighed and determined for a time and in part by such a kind father of equity and justice. But what we mournfully reply is that the intrigues and feigned deceptions of our enemies are worth more to his sanctity than our simple and pure defense; for with patience and equanimity, beyond the suffering of all our predecessors, we humbly submitted to our royal dignity, and to the divinely attributed power of that reverence, nay, rather, to the prince of the apostles, and more than could be believed, we appeared faithfully to the admonitions of our fathers, and following the various and manifold exhortations of his messengers for the sake of love God, and the reverence of the saints, in some of the themes of our region, we have exaggerated in part, otherwise than was necessary. Therefore, hoping, and believing in all ways, we trust in the most holy Pontiff for the help of our protection. But we do not know by what suggestions, or certainly by superfluous promises, that the unexpected delay gave birth to multiple similitudes; and for this reason our republic suffered no small injury. But we, incessantly proclaiming in letters and words, and repeating the same in different embassies, humbly demanded that we and our accusers, according to the divine and human laws, should merit the audience of his pontiff, as reason teaches, by presenting our presence. But as often as we were repulsed, even at last forced many times over, we placed our judgment and our refuge in that rock, of which the psalmist confidently said: The mountains of the high deer, the rock is the refuge of the hedgehog (Ps. 103).

Moreover, that above all clouded the line of our mind, that we are driven from the holy seat itself, whose progenitors and I have sworn to protect that holy mother Church, with divine help, piously and faithfully interceding. And indeed, beyond what can be done, we congratulate ourselves that the Bulgarians and other heathen savages are invited to the thresholds of the holy apostles, nay, that the holy Church, according to the prophecy of the prophet, enlarges the place of her tent, and makes her cords long, and stretches out the skins of her tabernacles (Isa. 54). But we are not a little sorry that we were not able to obtain the audience of your predecessor by so often yearning for it. But leaving these aside, let us return to the purpose of our minds, and the excellence of your apostolate worthy of God, and, as it is worthy, let us resound the glory to God on high, who looking forward to the most merciful condescension of the flock acquired by the rose of his own blood, your pontifical decree, by his election in the seat of the holy mother Church placed, for our salvation and that of the entire Christian people.

And since almighty God, chief of the shepherds, in that holy seat, exalted your pontificate to the pinnacle, we are prepared to present in all things the salutary aid of our serenity, for the defense, state, and honor of your pontificate, in the manner of our predecessors. And as a witness to the founder of all things, none of the Catholic kings, none of the Christian princes, desires to be more devoted to your sanctity, and more ready for your benefit, than our smallness. For if time has smiled, and with the help of divine clemency the scandals have subsided into slumber, which with the simultaneity and suggestion of our rivals, that is, the members of Satan, have enormously emerged, we long for your sight in many ways, and to be encouraged by your conversations worthy of God, and to receive a sweet blessing. Finally, we humbly beseech your almighty fatherhood not to prefer any one of royal dignity and name similar to us in any way, or to prefer our determined meekness, nor even to extend to us the tips of your beatitude, to direct it through someone, unless, either through our legate, or at least through you intended by your holy side, or by the message of the most august of our Germans, the Emperor Louis: for, let us truly confess, not a little shame has hitherto been known to have arisen in these parts by a deed of this kind, and unless it is carefully foreseen in the future, it may generate some kind of crisis.

In the meantime, let us beseech you all by all means, that, having assured our highness by your letters of your desirable prosperity, you deign to impart to us the gift of dear sonship, and by your abundant prayers present to the Lord a commendable and praiseworthy serenity for us, inasmuch as we have been supported by the pious prayers of such a great father, the government entrusted to us. By relying on Christ, let us be able to govern. May Almighty God bless your pontificate with splendor, and may he deign to keep the angelic sanctity safe for us for a long time. Amen.

THREE LETTERS

LATIN TEXT

EPISTOLA PRIMA. AD NICOLAUM PAPAM.

Conqueritur quod pontifex nimium de ipso ejus aemulis credat. Dolere se significat de Theutgaudi et Guntharii excommunicatione. Caeterum purgans se de omnibus, paratum se ostendit coram pontifice adversariorum calumnias refellere.

Domino vere beatissimo et sanctissimo totius sanctae Dei Ecclesiae summo pontifici et universali papae NICOLAO, LOTHARIUS, divina praeveniente clementia, rex, summae felicitatis ac praesentis prosperitatis pacem et gloriam.

Postquam nobis divina dignatio sua gratuita clementia regni gubernacula commisit, more praedecessorum nostrorum Christianissimorum regum, semper et in omnibus sublimandam beati Petri apostolorum principis sedem, ut dignum est, reverenter dileximus, atque instanter, quantum in nobis est, illam exaltare parati sumus, deque vestro tanquam summo spiritalis Patris regimine semper salubria haurire cupientes, veritatis voce vobis dictum recolimus: Petre, amas me? pasce oves meas (Joan. XI); et per prophetam: Ego pascam oves meas, dicit Dominus Deus: quod perierat requiram, et quod abjectum fuerat reducam, et quod confractum erat alligabo, et quod infirmum consolidabo (Ezech. XXXIV). Admodum quippe desideramus citius vobis nostram exhibere praesentiam, ut illud veriori experientia implere possitis, quod idem propheta post pauca subintulit: Et judicabo illas in judicio et justitia (Ibid.). Revera serenissimum ac devotissimum circa piam paternitatem vestram nostrae mentis affectum acriter obnubilat, quod aemulorum nostrorum falsidicis vocibus nimium creduli, ultra quam nobis necesse esset, in nostra derogatione sanctissimi apostolatus vestri aurem accommodatis. Praesertim cum nostra mansuetudo promptissima sit omni deroganti vera, et justa ratione resistere: quod et legati vestri, nuper in his partibus directi, vobis intimare poterant si vellent, quia nos data nostris accusatoribus firmitate aditum veniendi concessimus et rationabilem satisfactionem, tanquam in vestra patientia, ex vestro latere directis explere parati fuimus, nihil nostrae regiae dignitati faventes, sed quasi unus ex vilioribus personis, sacerdotalibus monitis parentes. Hoc totum nostri aemuli sinistra interpretatione intelligentes, exarserunt in concupiscentia regni nobis divina dignatione jure haereditario concessi: non attendentes Scripturam dicentem: Domini est regnum, et cuicunque voluerit dabit illud (Dan. IV): neque Apostolum dicentem: Non est potestas nisi a Deo (Rom. XIII). Illius ergo victrici dextera pro nobis, uti credimus, pugnante, qui novit et diripientem, et eum qui diripitur, parvipendimus eorum fucatas simultates: solummodo ut vestri pontificatus anchora, in solidissimo sanctae matris Ecclesiae fundamento fixa, nobis similiter petentibus concedere dignetur quod in mandatis digito Dei scriptis legitur: Juste judica proximo tuo (Lev. XIX). Porro nos in ultimis pene regni nostri finibus commorantes, et erga infestationem paganorum laboriosas excubias servantes, discurrentium relatione comperimus, Theutgaudum Trevirensem, et Guntharium Agrippinensem, a vestra auctoritate excommunicatos, atque oris proprii testimonio canonice damnatos: quod nos non sine gravi moerore haurientes, decrevimus longanimiter ac patienter ferre nuntiata, et ut olim in pluribus actum est, restitutionis spem habere, et pie refricatis ac retractatis omnibus, locum rationabilis misericordiae a vestra largitate praestolari. Interea accidit nobis nosse, quod Guntharius missarum solemnia antequam ad nos perveniret celebrare non metuit, et juxta praecedentem consuetudinem episcopale chrisma conficere, et Spiritum paracletum tradere praesumpsit: quod nos satis aegre tulimus, et ut hoc non fieret, tanquam mortiferum venenum, modis omnibus abominamur. Illo autem ad nos veniente, ejus missam audire noluimus, nec in aliquo illi communicare ratum duximus, et juxta Veritatis vocem, quasi scandalizantem oculum, a nobis eruere maculam disponimus, quousque sanctissimi apostolatus vestri finitivam sententiam de illo rescire valeamus. Epistolam quoque a vestra sanctitate episcopis dioeceseos directam illi transmisimus, ut ibidem canonicas atque apostolicas sanctiones liquido cognoscens, videat quid in posterum illi agendum sit. De caetero veraciter ac sinceriter vestra paternitas noverit, quod Theutgaudus simplicissimus atque innocentissimus vir, vestram humiliter ferens censuram, in nullo de sacro ministerio contingere praesumpsit, magis eligens dehonorationem praesentialiter in oculis hominum pati, quam per inobedientiam ab illius membris secerni, qui caput est humilium, suisque discipulis ait: Discite a me quia mitis sum et humilis corde, et invenietis requiem animabus vestris (Matth. XI). Ipse enim, qui superbis resistit, et gratiam praestat humilibus, poterit illum, si innocens est, de supernis misericorditer respicere. Enimvero legatis nostris Theutgaudo et Gunthario, nihil tale aliquid in sua legatione fari praecipimus, unde damnationis notam incurrerent. Sed nec de Ingeltrude uxore Bosonis aliquod praejudicium ferre debemus aut volumus: quam nos, comperto quod anathematis vinculo esset innodata, Gunthario, quia tunc in sua parochia erat, commendavimus, monentes, ut de illa suum ministerium faceret, imo illam ex omnibus regni nostri finibus eliminandam censuimus. Legati enim vestri illam postmodum requirentes, atque in medio statuentes, nos ignoramus quem finem causae ipsius imposuerint. Episcopi vero dioeceseos Trevirensis metropolis, et Agrippinae Coloniae, nec complices damnatorum, nec fautores vitiorum, nec in aliquo apostolicorum decretorum contemptores, vel canonicorum dogmatum violatores esse probabuntur, sed sanae atque catholicae fidei ac veri Dei cultores. Igitur propter Deum, sanctam et individuam Trinitatem, humiliter petimus, ut facile criminosos ad causationem nostram nullatenus admittatis: neque ut Apostolus docet, omni spiritui credatis, sed probate si ex Deo sit (I Joan. IV): quia parati sumus, si ratio dictaverit, per nosmetipsos polire, quod aemulorum invidia fingit aliena. Omnipotens Deus sanctissimum praesulatus vestri apicem aequitatis lance moderatum diu incolumem custodiat. Amen.

EPISTOLA II. AD EUMDEM. Ut excommunicationem ob consortium cum Waldrada comminatam effugiat, suum ad Nicolaum Romam adventum nuntiat, et ut eum spe bona ludificet episcoporum ad eumdem legationem decernit, et auxilium contra Saracenos, si opus sit, ei pollicetur.

Domino vere sanctissimo ac beatissimo, totiusque Dei Ecclesiae roseo pii Regis Christi sanguine acquisitae summo pontifici et universali papae NICOLAO, LOTHARIUS, divina propitiante clementia rex ac devotissimus filius vester, sempiternam cum gaudio, prosperitatis, et felicitatis gloriam, fideleque servitium.

Rex regum et princeps pastorum Christus, qui sacerdotalem, et regiam dignitatem in ministerio nostro redemptionis in seipso univit, quique sui ovilis curam beato Petro apostolorum principi tuendam commisit, ille nos salubribus edictis instituit, ut apostolatus vestri sacratissimum apicem divinitus in fundamento Ecclesiae sublimatum fideliter diligamus, et humiliter veneremur. Hinc est, quod nostrae mansuetudinis affectus, circa vestram celsitudinem verae charitatis igne inflammatur, et a multis jam retro diebus, nos ad vestram praesentiam desiderabiliter invitare non cessat. Quapropter hos vestrae eminentissimae paternitati direximus apices, ut de vestra optabili sospitate celerius rescire possimus, quae omnium gemmarum nitore pretiosior, omnique thesauro charior nostro amplexatur in corpore. Et quia nos hoc idem de vestra sanitate incunctanter credimus, satius vobis intimandum decrevimus, quod divina opitulante clementia, nostra mansuetudo optime viget, fideliumque nostrorum generalitas in necessariis reipublicae negotiis, opitulante Christo, salubribus proficit incrementis, imo prosperitatis successum ab ipso bonorum omnium largitore profuturum humiliter ac fideliter praestolamur. Regnum quoque nobis divina pietate commissum ab omni paganorum infestatione, aliorumque inimicorum depraedatione, dextera omnipotentis Dei pro nobis pugnante, et auxiliantibus meritis beati Petri apostoli, vestrisque precibus almifluis suffragantibus, hactenus cum omni integritate tutum manere cognoscite.

Porro vestrae sanctitatis noverit pia paternitas, quod isto tempore ferventissimum desiderium habemus causa orationis apostolorum limina visitare, vestramque diu desideratam faciem cernere, et sacra dulciter amplexari vestigia; et jam secundo, ac tertio nostri itineris apparatum sub certa deliberatione repetitum habemus, quod in voto manet implere desiderantes. Verum si aliqua, quod absit, periculosorum temporum varietas votum nostrum interceperit, legatos nostros Gutfridum [Luitfridum] dilectissimum avunculum nostrum, et Waltarium fidelem nostrum, necnon et Theutgaudum venerabilem archiepiscopum, atque Attonem [Hattonem, puta Viridunensis Ecclesiae] coepiscopum ad vestram praesentiam destinare procurabimus, ut per illos liquido cognoscat vestra celsitudo, quam fideles vobis per omnia existimus, nos et fideles nostri, et quam fideliter vestris salubribus consiliis, et spiritualibus monitis parere desideramus. Revera sicut spiritalis ac devotissimus filius reverentissimo patri, atque universali papae, debet, quippe nos et venerabiles episcopi atque fideles nostri, si non corpore, corde tamen ad vestra sacra vestigia provoluti, humiliter petimus, ut si aliquis inimicorum nostrorum ex nostra parte, quiddam sinistrum mendoso falsitatis elogio vestris sanctissimis auribus significare praesumpserit, quasi serpentinum virus, apostolica abominetur auctoritas. Et quidem nostri episcopi veritatis discipuli, magistri erroris esse non possunt, qui orthodoxi patris catholicae et apostolicae fidei veri probabuntur esse cultores.

Inter ista vero ratum esse duximus inserendum, quod si aliqua incursio paganorum fines beati Petri vobis coelitus commissos adire tentaverit, aut forte terminos augustissimi imperatoris atque amantissimi germani nostri Ludovici, prout nuperrima atque infausta relatione comperimus, irrumpere praesumpserit, illud nobis absque ulla dilatione ocius significari deposcimus; quia quolibet postposito rerum temporalium damno, atque parvipenso perituri discrimine regni pro amore, et timore Dei, et beatorum apostolorum, sanctorumque omnium reverentia, simulque vestra sanctissima paternitate, quam prae omnibus mortalibus diligere, ac venerari decrevimus, nos ac fideles nostros morti, ac periculo tradere parati sumus, scientes esse scriptum: Timere non debemus mortem, quae sine dubio perducit ad vitam.

Igitur quibus valemus votis, Domini misericordiam imploramus, ut nostram mansuetudinem vestrae excellentissimae almitati tandem repraesentet incolumen; quatenus verior experientia apostolatus vestri puriter cognoscat, utrum prolata a veritatis fonte emanaverint. Omnipotens Deus nostri memorem summum vestri sanctissimi pontificatus apicem prosperis successibus feliciter insignitum ad custodiam gregis conservare, et exaltare di etur, gloriosissime, ac praestantissime pater.

EPISTOLA III. AD ADRIANUM II PAPAM De Nicolai obitu certior factus Lotharius, has litteras ad ejus successorem Adrianum scribit, rogans ut quod a Nicolao obtinere non potuit, ab eo impetraret, suum Romae adventum.

Sanctissimo et perbeatissimo HADRIANO summo pontifici et universali papae, LOTHARIUS, divina praeveniente clementia, rex, aeternae beatitudinis et praesentis prosperitatis pacem et gloriam.

Infausta relatio, et in ambiguo hactenus manens, ut ita dicamus, acriter nostrae serenitatis transverberavit aures intimando, quod beatae memoriae domnus Nicolaus universalis papa ab hac lacrymarum valle, vocante Christo, decesserit, cum sanctis, ut credimus, inaestimabiliter coronandus. Unde nostrae mansuetudinis affectio admodum ingemiscens, gemino dolore concutitur, videlicet quod mater omnium Ecclesiarum Dei, sancta, et apostolica Ecclesia, tali ac tanto caruit patre, atque in coelesti Jerusalem lucerna ardens et lucens nostris periculosis temporibus a tenebrosis malefidis Dei [diei] finibus sit remota. Nec differt, ut omnis Christiana religio de tanto pontifice doleat, et omnis ordo ecclesiasticus de prudentissimo ac sanctissimo papa ingemiscat. Revera nos potius deflemus, qui causas nostrae calumniae insolentes, et fraudulentas aemulorum nostrorum querimonias, tam benigno patri aequitatis, et justitiae lance ponderandas ac determinandas ad tempus et in parte commisimus. Sed quod lugubriter replicamus, plus apud sanctitatem illius valuere nostrorum inimicorum insidiae et simulatae deceptiones, quam nostra simplex et pura defensio; quippe patienter atque aequanimiter ultra sufferentiam omnium praedecessorum nostrorum nostram regiam dignitatem, ac divinitus attributam potestatem reverentiae illius, imo potius apostolorum principis, humiliter submisimus, et ultra quam credi posset, suis paternis monitis fidenter paruimus, ac missorum suorum varia et multiplicia hortamenta sectando propter amorem Dei, et reverentiam sanctorum, in aliquibus a nostro regio themate, secus quam oporteret in parte exorbitavimus. Igitur sperantes, et modis omnibus credentes, in sanctissimo pontifice fidum nostrae tuitionis auxilium ponimus. Sed nescimus quibus suggestionibus, aut certe superfluis promissionibus actum est, quod insperata dilatio multiplices peperit simultates; atque ob hoc nostra respublica non modicam usquequaque pertulit laesionem. Nos autem litteris et verbis indesinenter proclamantes, et diversis legationibus eadem repetentes, humiliter postulavimus, ut nos et accusatores nostri juxta divinas et humanas leges, sui pontificii audientiam mereremur, ut ratio docet, nostram praesentiam exhibendo. Sed toties repulsi etiam tandem multipliciter coacti, judicium ac refugium nostrum, in illa collocavimus petra, de qua Psalmista confidens aiebat: Montes excelsi cervis, petra petra refugium erinacei (Psal. CIII).

Porro illud potissimum nostrae mentis aciem obnubilavit, quod nos ab ipsa sancta sede repellimur, quorum progenitores et atavi illam sanctam matrem Ecclesiam, divino auxilio pie ac fideliter patrocinantes protexere. Et quidem ultra quam fari possit, congratulamur, quod Bulgaros, et alia paganorum feritas ad limina sanctorum apostolorum invitatur, imo quod sancta Ecclesia, juxta vaticinium prophetae, dilatat locum tentorii sui, et longos facit funiculos suos, ac pelles tabernaculorum suorum extendit (Isa. LIV). Sed non modice contristamur, quod tam crebro illuc anhelando audientia praedecessoris vestri potiri non valuimus. Sed his omissis, ad nostrae mentis propositum, et vestri Deo digni apostolatus excellentiam redeamus, et uti dignum est, gloriam in excelsis Deo resonemus, qui roseo proprii sanguinis pretio acquisito gregi misericordissima dignatione prospiciens, vestri pontificii jubar, sua electione in sede sanctae matris Ecclesiae collocavit, ad nostram et totius Christianae plebis salutem.

Et quia omnipotens Deus princeps pastorum, in illa sancta sede, vestri pontificatus apicem sublimavit, nostrae serenitatis salubre auxilium, ad defensionem, statum, atque honorem pontificatus vestri, more praedecessorum nostrorum, in omnibus exhibere parati sumus. Et teste rerum omnium conditore, nullus catholicorum regum, nullus Christianorum principum devotior vestrae sanctitati, et promptior vestrae utilitati esse desiderat, quam nostra exiguitas [al. quantitas]. Nam si tempus arriserit, et auxiliante divina clementia scandala sopita conquieverint, quae simultate et suggestione aemulorum nostrorum, membrorum videlicet Satanae, enormiter emersere, vestrum multipliciter desideramus conspectum, et vestris Deo dignis animari colloquiis, atque melliflua benedictione potiri. Denique almifluam paternitatem vestram humiliter precamur, ut nullum regiae dignitatis, et nominis nobis consimilem praeferre quoquo modo, aut praeponere nostrae mansuetudini decernatis, neque etiam apices beatitudinis vestrae nobis porrigendos, per aliquem dirigere placeat, nisi, aut per nostrum legatum, aut certe per vestrum a vestro sancto latere destinatum, vel per nuntium augustissimi germani nostri Ludovici imperatoris: quia, ut vere fateamur, non modica simultas hactenus istis in partibus per hujusmodi factum orta noscitur, et nisi in posterum caute praevisum fuerit, quoddam poterit generare discrimen.

Interea modis omnibus obsecramus, ut de vestra optabili prosperitate litteris vestris celsitudinem nostram certam reddentes, charae filiationis munus nobis impertiri dignemini, et vestris almifluis precibus nostram apud Dominum commendabilem atque veniabilem exhibeatis serenitatem, quatenus tanti patris piis precibus suffulti, creditum nobis regimen. Christo opitulante, gubernare valeamus. Omnipotens Deus vestri pontificii splendifluum jubar, atque angelicam sanctimoniam diu nobis incolumem conservare dignetur. Amen.

THREE LETTERS

The Scriptorium Project is the work of a small group of lay people of various apostolic churches who are interested in the preservation, transmission, and translation of the works of the early and medieval church. Our efforts are to make the works of the church fathers accessible to anyone who might have an interest in Christian antiquities and the theological, philosophical, and moral writings that have become the bedrock of Western Civilization.

To-date, our releases have pulled from the Greek, Syriac, Georgian, Latin, Celtic, Ethiopian, and Coptic traditions of Christianity, and have been pulled from sundry local traditions and languages.

THREE LETTERS

Other Selections from the Early Frankish Church Series:

Letter to Brunhilda of Austrasia by St. Germain of Paris (Sept. 2010)
The Spiritual Combat by St. Bernard of Clairvaux (Dec. 2010)
In Praise of the New Chivalry by St. Bernard of Clairvaux (Jan. 2011)
Three Letters by Lothair, Holy Roman Emperor Mar. 2011)
Testament by St. Burgundofara the Abbess (Jan. 2016)
Laws of the Monastery and the Church by Theuderic III, King of Franks (Feb. 2016)
The Life of King Sigebert II by Sigebert of Gembloux (Mar. 2016)
Two Letters from a Gallic Patrician by Dynamius the Patrician (July 2016)
Life of St. Germain by St. Venantius Fortunatus (Aug. 2016)
Three Letters from the Companion of the Bulgars by St. Rupert of Juvavum (Aug. 2017)
An Account of the Gallican Liturgy by St. Germain of Paris (June 2018)
Preludes by Photius of Paris (Nov. 2018)
The Privileges of Rome by Louis I the Pious, Frankish Emperor (Apr. 2019)
Edicts of the Synod of Paris by Chlothar II, King of Franks (Aug. 2019)
Laws of the Church (Ecclesiasticae Praeceptiones) by Chlothar III, King of Franks (Apr. 2020)
Laws of the Church (Ecclesiasticae Praeceptiones) by St. Dagobert II, King of Franks (Sept. 2020)
Letters of Paulinus by St. Paulinus of Aquileia (Aug. 2021)
The Italian Diplomas by Charlemagne, Holy Roman Emperor (Apr. 2023)

THREE LETTERS

www.ingramcontent.com/pod-product-compliance
Lightning Source LLC
LaVergne TN
LVHW021240080526
838199LV00088B/5415